The Science of Brain-Computer Interfaces

Melding Mind and Machine

Table of Contents

Chapter 1. Introduction

In this Special Report, we explore the invaluable realm of Brain-Computer Interfaces (BCIs), a fascinating fusion of neurology, computer science, and biomedical engineering. Despite sounding like sci-fi brought to life, BCIs serve a critical role in enhancing human cognition, communication, and sensory motor systems. But you don't need to be a scientist to understand this cutting-edge field. Our report breaks down the exquisite science behind BCIs in a straightforward manner, demystifying complex jargon and focusing on the aspects that matter. As we unpack this progressive technology from its humble beginnings to its groundbreaking applications in neuroprosthetics, potential future trends, and ethical considerations, we slowly but surely immerse ourselves in the astounding world where mind and machine become one. Venture with us into the intriguing union of biology and technology, where not only is the future written, but also humanity embarks on a journey resolutely ensnared in the syntheses of imagination and invention.

Chapter 2. The Dawn of Brain-Computer Interfaces

From speculative fictions to earnest hypotheses of pioneering scientists, the advent of Brain-Computer Interfaces (BCIs) can be traced back to the distant past when man first dreamt of augmenting human capabilities. However, it wasn't until the late 20th century that these dreams began to materialize into concrete studies and experiments, which ultimately bore the fruits known today as Brain-Computer Interfaces. This chapter traverses the intricate journey of BCIs, starting from theoretical foundations laid by early visionary scholars to practical realizations in neurology, computer science, and biomedical engineering.

2.1. The Visionaries

In the early days of BCI research, the concept was merely a distant vision kindled by a handful of visionary scientists predicting a future where humankind would be interfaced with technology. One such pioneer, J.C.R. Licklider - often hailed as the 'Johnny Appleseed' of computing - proposed a symbiotic relationship between humans and machines in his seminal paper "Man-Computer Symbiosis" back in 1960.

Licklider theorized a paradigm where humans and computers worked cooperatively, leveraging each other's strengths and compensating for each other's weaknesses. His vision sparked a thought revolution that cascaded through the decades, inspiring generations of researchers and scientists, ultimately laying the bedrocks of current BCI technology.

2.2. The Birth of Paralleled Research Pathways

The first half of the 20th century saw parallel foundational research in two distinct but interconnected fields: neuroscience and computing technology. On one side, neurologists like Wilder Penfield were making groundbreaking discoveries about brain functionality, mapping human brains and unveiling heretofore unknown capabilities and characteristics.

Concurrently, advancements in computing technology, such as the introduction of the first programmable digital computer during World War II and the development of the transistor in the late 1940s, ushered in the digital age. This combination of understanding the human brain coupled with advances in computer technology set the stage for the development of BCIs.

2.3. From Theory to Practice: Initial Experimentations

In the 1970s, the concept of BCIs started to morph from theory into practice. The pioneering research on neurofeedback conducted by researchers at UCLA under the guidance of Dr. Barry Sterman was instrumental in this transition. Sterman's work on EEG and neurofeedback provided a foundational understanding of how human brains could control certain activities on the computer screen solely through brain waves.

Another key development during this era was the conceptualization of P300-based BCIs by Farwell and Donchin in 1988. They discovered a specific event-related potential in EEG signals, termed the P300 waveform, which indicated a recognition response in the brain. This wave could be harnessed to command a computer through focused attention.

2.4. Technological Advances: Fine-tuning the Systems

As we moved into the 21st century, the technology underpinning BCIs saw significant refinement and advancement. With improved signal processing algorithms and machine learning techniques, researchers started to realize the true potential of BCIs. Techniques like machine learning and Deep Neural Networks allowed for greater accuracy in translating brain signals into executable commands.

Simultaneously, developments in sensor technology such as dry-electrode and noninvasive scanning technologies were instrumental in building user-friendly and nonintrusive BCI systems, broadening the appeal and adaptability of the technology for mainstream uses.

2.5. The Dawn of Practical Applications

The last decade has witnessed an exponential rise in practical applications of BCI technology. From neuroprosthetics aiding amputees to regain motor function, to assistive technologies for people with severe physical disabilities, the impact of BCIs in changing lives is more pronounced than ever. Innovative ventures like Elon Musk's Neuralink aim to popularize BCI technology by making it more accessible and user-friendly, even envisioning a future where BCIs may enhance cognitive abilities of the healthy individuals as well.

While the journey of BCIs from dream to reality has been one of incredible vision, tenacious research, and technological leaps, it is still marked by challenges pertaining to accuracy, usability, and ethical considerations. As we step further into this sci-fi made reality, a future where mind and machine work synergistically could be more than just a distant dream. The dawn of BCIs represents a critical juncture in our evolutionary journey - where biology and technology meld, rewriting the rules of what it means to be human.

Chapter 3. Decoding the Mind: How BCIs Read Brain Activity

Brain-Computer Interfaces (BCIs) operate based on our understanding of how the brain functions. The human brain, a complex network of approximately 86 billion neurons, is continuously active, even in sleep. They communicate through a sequence of electrical pulses popularly known as 'brain waves' or 'neural oscillations', carrying information through an intricate web of neural pathways. By tapping into this wealth of information, BCIs can act as a bridge between the human brain and external devices.

3.1. Uncovering the Basics of Brain Signals

Detecting and interpreting these electrical signals is a crucial first step in building BCIs. There are different tools to measure these signals, with each tool varying in its invasiveness, spatial resolution, and temporal resolution. Electroencephalography (EEG), for instance, uses electrodes placed on the scalp to measure the brain's electrical activity, offering high temporal resolution but relatively low spatial resolution. In contrast, technologies such as functional Magnetic Resonance Imaging (fMRI) offer much higher spatial resolution, capturing detailed activity patterns across the brain, but trail EEG in temporal resolution.

Let's explore in detail how these different technologies decode brain signals, and thus how BCIs read the human mind.

3.2. Electroencephalography (EEG)

EEG is the most commonly used technique for reading brain activity in BCIs. It detects electrical activity via electrodes placed along the scalp. These electrodes are designed to pick up electric potential changes resulting from synchronous neuronal activity within the brain. The benefit of EEG is its unparalleled temporal resolution (on the order of milliseconds), which allows BCIs to respond in real time to a user's thoughts or reactions.

EEG-based BCIs uniquely harness different types of EEG rhythms, such as Alpha, Beta, Gamma, Delta, and Theta waves. Each rhythm corresponds to different states of consciousness or cognitive activities. For instance, Alpha waves are dominant during relaxed and calm states, while Beta waves are associated with active thinking or focus.

3.3. Magnetoencephalography (MEG)

While similar in many respects to EEG, MEG detects the magnetic fields generated by electrical currents in the brain. This method offers a superior signal-to-noise ratio compared to EEG and gives a more accurate source localization. Still, MEG systems are bulky and expensive, limiting their widespread use in separate BCI applications.

3.4. Functional Magnetic Resonance Imaging (fMRI)

fMRI records brain signals by detecting changes in blood oxygenation – a method known as Blood Oxygenation Level Dependent (BOLD) signals. When a brain area is active, it demands more oxygen, leading to an increase in incoming oxygenated blood flow. BOLD signals provide a sophisticated insight into the location of brain activity, allowing for detailed spatial mapping.

One disadvantage of fMRI, however, is its poor temporal resolution. The delay in blood flow changes relative to neuronal activity, combined with the scanner's slow sampling rate, makes real-time applications challenging.

3.5. Electrocorticography (ECoG)

ECoG straddles the line between invasive and non-invasive techniques, measuring electrical activity from the cerebral cortex through electrodes placed directly on the brain's surface. While this approach requires surgery and carries risks, it provides both excellent temporal and spatial resolution, making it a powerful tool for BCIs, particularly in medical applications.

3.6. Invasive Techniques

While non-invasive techniques have many advantages, invasive techniques, such as recording from single neurons or groups of neurons using implanted electrodes, can provide unparalleled resolution and precision. However, the added risk and ethical implications of these procedures limit their application.

3.7. Interpreting Neural Signals

Regardless of the signal acquisition method, BCI systems must interpret the acquired data. This interpretation is achieved via various signal processing and machine learning techniques that analyze frequencies, amplitudes, and phases of the observed brain signals.

Signal interpretation often employs advanced algorithms involving pattern recognition, neural networks, and adaptive modeling. These algorithms enable the BCI to find correlations between particular patterns in neural activity and specific thoughts or commands. Through training, BCIs can refine this process, improving their ability to understand the user's intention from the captured signals.

3.8. Future Reading Techniques

The future of decoding brain signals for BCI use looks promising. Plans are in the works to leverage newer artificial intelligence and machine learning algorithms for more accurate and efficient signal interpretation. Furthermore, advancements in nanotechnology could lead to the development of even less invasive yet high-resolution signal acquisition methods.

In summary, BCIs stand at the forefront in the quest to understand both the workings of individual neurons and their collective function across intricate neural networks. They symbolize an exceptional marriage of biotechnology and computation, promising to revolutionize how we communicate, interact, and even perceive our own consciousness.

However, as with any emerging technology, BCIs bring to the fore new ethical challenges. While these technologies may mark progress in our understanding of the human brain, they also raise questions about privacy, identity, and the very essence of human cognition. Despite these concerns, the potential benefits of BCI technology far outweigh its possible risks, marking it as a crucial avenue of future scientific exploration.

Chapter 4. Translating Thoughts into Action: How BCIs Communicate with Computers

To dive into the fascinating workings of Brain-Computer Interfaces (BCIs), we need to elucidate how they manage to translate our thoughts into commands that a computer can understand and execute. This magical journey involves intricacies of the flesh and silicon working together seamlessly, turning science into almost an art form. This translation process involves multiple stages and is carefully orchestrated by an amalgamation of sophisticated software and hardware.

4.1. The Basics of Brain Signals

Everything starts with our brain. It's an intricate network of billions of neurons, with each responsible for generating electrical signals. These signals collaborate to control everything, right from our most rudimentary involuntary reflexes to executing our deepest cognitive thoughts. Moreover, their myriad colorations and frequencies vary depending on our thought processes, mood, or the task at hand.

These electrical signals, or brain waves, are detected using an electroencephalography (EEG) method. The EEG device uses electrodes positioned on the scalp, which are capable of picking up the brain's faint electrical whispers. The strength of these signals depends largely on the depth of the neurons firing them; signals from superficial cortical neurons are substantial and easier to pick up compared to those emitted from deeper areas like the thalamus.

4.2. From Brainwaves to Binary

Upon capture by the EEG device, the raw brain signals are anything but coherent to computers. They are riddled with extraneous noise and unwanted signals, colloquially termed 'artifacts,' such as those produced when we blink, swallow or during muscle contractions.

Signal processing algorithms step in here, filtering out these artifacts and ensuring only pure, untainted brain signals are detected. They enhance the signal-to-noise ratio, converting the raw EEG data into an oscillation of discrete waves, each with distinct amplitudes and frequencies.

This cleaned brainwave data then gets digitized. In essence, this translates the analog signal (the brainwaves) into a digital format—a language that computers can understand: the language of binary, consisting only of zeros and ones.

4.3. Command Generation

Once translated into binary, the signal needs to be interpreted. To interact with a BCI, users have to manipulate their brain waves intentionally. This manipulation is often realized by moving body parts or performing cognitive tasks like doing mental arithmetic. The changes in brainwave amplitudes and frequencies, captured while a user performs tasks, are then matched with specific functions or commands.

Most BCIs use machine learning algorithms to catch patterns in the brainwave signals and correlate them with respective commands. With enough practice, users can learn to regulate their brain waves deliberately to initiate specific commands, much akin to how one learns to ride a bicycle. And like riding a bicycle, it gets easier with practice.

4.4. Real-Time Performance and Feedback

BCIs need to operate in real time for effective user interaction. Quick and accurate command execution based on received signals is crucial to create a smooth user experience. BCIs today can implement feedback mechanisms where users can adjust their strategy depending on the system's output, a procedure termed biofeedback. That way, users continually improve, perfecting their ability to control the interface over time.

4.5. Bridging the Gap between Man and Machine

Therefore, the seamless conversation between brains and computers occurs through robust signal capturing, careful preprocessing, binary translation, command generation, and real-time command execution. The BCI captures the body's internal dialogue, translates the neurochemical language into digital lingo, and communicates this 'thought' to the computer. Voila, the computer then executes the intended function.

4.6. BCIs: A Continuous Learning Process

A consistent point to note is that BCIs learn along with their user. They consistently retrain, i.e., learn from adjustments made by the user, and improve their own performance in understanding and interpreting user brainwave patterns. This continual learning and adaptation offer a personalized BCI experience.

As we conclude this chapter, it becomes clear that what seemed like an inscrutable maze of signal processing is nothing but a systematic and methodical translation process. BCIs today have begun to bridge the chasm between the organic and the electronic, promising an exciting tomorrow where limits for man-machine interface keep extending, spurred on by curiosity, research, technology, and innovation.

Chapter 5. Case Studies: BCIs in Action

Apropos of the daunting yet thrilling task to unravel the machinations of the human brain, Brain-Computer Interfaces (BCIs) have forged an avenue bound only by the limits of human ingenuity, prompting monumental strides in diverse fields. This chapter delves into three compelling case studies that illuminate the tangible benefits of BCIs, from aiding patients with paralysis to improving cognitive performance and exploring the thrilling potential for augmented human capability.

5.1. Exploring Therapeutic Horizons: The Story of Cathy Hutchinson

In a groundbreaking endeavor that bears testimony to the power of BCI, Cathy Hutchinson, a stroke survivor paralyzed from the neck down, was equipped with a BCI system called BrainGate, arguably one of the best-documented BCIs in history. Developed by Brown University researchers, BrainGate is an aspirational project evinced by a multi-electrode array implanted into the patient's motor cortex, the part of the brain involved in planning, control, and execution of voluntary movements.

The matrix of tiny electrodes picks up electric signals produced by brain activity which, in turn, are transmitted to an external device translating these signals into control commands. In Cathy's case, it enabled her to control a robotic arm just by thinking - an unimaginable feat that, for the first time in nearly 15 years of complete paralysis, allowed her to sip coffee independently – drawing an invigorated focus on what might be in the offing for BCIs.

5.2. Boosting Cognitive Capacities: The Frontier of Learning Enhancement

Venturing into the realm of cognitive enhancement, a riveting case study revolves around the concept of neurofeedback training using BCIs. In one experiment conducted on students in a learning environment, a BCI system was employed to monitor their brainwave activities during study sessions. Through this exercise, researchers were able to decipher when the brain was most receptive to learning based on the type and intensity of frequencies generated.

In the course of the next phase, participants were provided with real-time feedback on their brain activity with instructions to induce a mental state conducive to optimal learning. This BCI-driven brain modulation led to a marked improvement in attention spans, recall abilities, and overall academic performance. This conspicuous affirmation of the potential of BCIs in enhancing cognitive capacities leads us to a speculative domain where we might harness the brain's raw power to optimize human potential for learning.

5.3. The Augmented Human: BCIs and Virtual Reality

As our final case study, we broach the boundary-pushing fusion of BCIs with Virtual Reality (VR), a fascinating arena that piquots on the interdisciplinary cohesion of neuroengineering, computer science, and immersive technology. Experimental projects in this field often involve controlling a VR avatar or navigating VR environments using only the power of thought – a clear exemplifier of BCI's transcendence beyond therapeutic contexts to recreational and futuristic scenarios.

In one such trailblazing experiment, participants with BCI-enabled headsets were able to fly a virtual drone through a 3D digital landscape. The brain signals related to the intention of movement were decoded by the BCI and translated into commands that controlled the drone. This potent combination of VR and BCI not only constructs the foundation for a new era of gaming but also unlocks speculative potentials such as virtual training environments for physical rehabilitation or piloting drones in real-world search and rescue missions.

These three case studies, demanding applause for their innovation, affirm the transformative potential inherent in BCIs. Braving new frontiers, these cases contribute constructive insights to our understanding of the brain, cognition, and motor control while advancing the pursuit of optimizing human potential in ways unimaginable prior to this technological revelation. The road towards this future is fraught with challenges, yet the allure of this remarkable fusion of neurology and technology fires the human imagination with an irresistible determination to not only unravel the mysteries of the brain but also bridge the gap between man and machine.

Chapter 6. Neuroprosthetics: The Gift of Mobility

The field of neuroprosthetics, particularly in relation to mobility, paints a powerful picture of how technology, when intertwined with the human body, can overcome biological limitations and give humans a second chance at normalcy. This involves harnessing the power of the mind in concert with the marvels of technology, bringing forth a symphony of biology and engineering that aspires to transform lives.

6.1. The Quest for Mobility

The majority of neuroprosthetic applications are aimed at restoring some form of sensory motor capabilities to individuals who have lost them due to accidents, illnesses, or inborn conditions. These individuals are often left with a significantly reduced quality of life, suffused with challenges that range from simple day-to-day activities to the more complex tasks that most of us take for granted. The function of neuroprosthetics is to help these people regain their autonomy, their dignity, and their joy of living.

Motor neuroprosthetics work on a rather simple, yet incredibly intricate principle. The device is designed to interface with the user's nervous system, taking electrical signals from the brain, interpreting them, and then employing these signals to control a prosthetic device. This could be anything from an artificial limb that helps a person walk, grasp, hold or swing, to a wheelchair that moves according to the patient's thoughts.

6.2. The Intricate Architecture of Neuroprosthetics

This magic of movement does not happen by chance; it requires an elaborate architecture that is tuned to not only accept input from the nervous system, but to also provide a seamless, natural response. First in line is the detection of the signals that the brain sends out. This is achieved via electrodes that are either non-invasively placed on the scalp (EEG), or more directly on the brain surface (ECoG), or inserted into the brain tissue (intracortical).

Once signals are detected, they need to be decoded - a task that's easier said than done. The brain is a maze of electric signals, with each tiny spot producing an array of signals depending on what the person wants their body to do. Deciphering these signals accurately is probably the most challenging aspect of neuroprosthetics.

Working to this end, researchers use machine learning algorithms to study patterns and learn from the user's brain signals. They teach these algorithms what each signal means by correlating the detected signals to actual or intended movements. With time, the algorithm gets better at translating brain signals into concrete actions.

The processed signals are then used to drive the mechanical prosthetic. Depending on the complexity, intricacy, and fineness of the prosthetic, the machine part can mimic human movement nearly perfectly. This incredibly orchestrated series of processes, from thought to action, enable a seamless interaction between human and machine, literally bringing thoughts to life.

6.3. Current Applications and Success Stories

Over the years, countless individuals have benefited from

neuroprosthetics, gaining independence and gaining a renewed sense of self. From simple artificial limbs to more sophisticated prosthetics such as the DEKA Arm (also known as the 'Luke Skywalker' arm) or thought-controlled wheelchairs, neuroprosthetics have made the unimaginable possible.

In 2012, Jan Scheuermann, paralyzed from the neck down, navigated a robotic arm solely with her thoughts to shake hands and stack cones. In 2014, a BCI recorded signals from the motor cortex of a paralyzed man and sent them to a sleeve on his arm, stimulating muscles and allowing him to lift a cup to his mouth, and drink from a straw.

More recently, advancements have extended to neuroprosthetics that offer sensory feedback. By providing the user with a sense of touch, pressure, or even temperature, these devices are making the interaction seem ever more natural.

6.4. Future Directions and Challenges

Like any other field of study, neuroprosthetics is not without its challenges. There is, as yet, no one-size-fits-all solution, and devices must be customized for each individual user. Interpreting the brain's complex language with precision remains a daunting task. Furthermore, achieving smooth, fine-tuned movement is often a stark challenge due to the raw nature of mechanics as compared to the fluidity of biological movement.

However, the future of neuroprosthetics is promising, with research trending toward implants that communicate wirelessly, eliminating the need for hard wires between the brain and the machine. Moreover, the expansion of machine learning and big data capabilities is significantly propelling advancements in decoding brain signals.

There also lies an audacious ambition to move beyond restoring lost functions. As the nuances of the brain's electrical language are further deciphered, there is the potential to tap into other brain networks tied to memory, learning, or even mood, opening vast, untouched horizons, reshaping individuals' experiences, and challenging our perspective of reality.

6.5. The Balance of Ethics

The field of neuroprosthetics is steeped in ethical considerations that are capturing the attention of academia and the public alike. As it stands at the intersection of medicine, engineering, and neuroscience, it raises questions about privacy, consent, and even identity.

Making sure these devices are accessible to those who need them, avoiding social disparities, is another essential concern. Justice in distribution, user safety, and preventions of misuse are other significant aspects that need addressing. Thus, while the science evolves, it must do so in tune with ethical and societal considerations, successfully harmonizing the symphony of biology, technology, and society.

Neuroprosthetics is a field that illuminates the extraordinary within the quotidian, imbuing mundane tasks with a sense of marvel - that of turning thoughts into reality. As we continue unraveling the mind's complex language and manipulating technology to match its rhythm, we are not only offering the gift of mobility, but also paving the path toward an era where the human mind's potential is truly unleashed.

Chapter 7. Technological Innovations: The Evolution of BCIs

Technology in the field of Brain-Computer Interfaces (BCIs) has undergone vast methodologies and modifications throughout the past decades. What began as an ideological venture into the fascinating cocktail of biology and technology has turned into a full-fledged discipline that continually churns out riveting developments.

7.1. The Dawn of BCIs

The inception of Brain-Computer Interfaces can be traced back to the 1970s, when Jacques Vidal, a pioneer in the field, proposed a concept that the electrical signals generated by the brain can be interpreted and controlled by a computer. However, the first rudimentary BCI was created by Eberhard Fetz in 1969. He demonstrated that monkeys could control a simple biofeedback meter while the monkeys' brain activity was recorded via biofeedback.

This event could be aptly termed the "Big Bang" of the BCI domain. Yet, the early BCIs were primarily restricted to research laboratories chiefly due to their large, unwieldy designs and the need for user training. Despite these constraints, the foundations for modern BCIs had been laid, and slowly but surely, the seeds of future innovation were beginning to sprout.

7.2. Technological Renaissance in BCIs

The advent of microcomputers and the increasing sophistication of neural recording techniques in the 1980s and '90s kindled a renaissance in BCI technology. Laboratories around the globe started concentrating their efforts on real-time analysis and interpretation of brain activity.

BCI technology went through staggering advancements with the advent of electroencephalography (EEG) and event-related potentials (ERPs). This discovery prompted a significant shift towards non-invasive techniques that offer real-time connectivity between the brain and computing devices without requiring a physical connection.

Also noteworthy is the onset of advanced machine learning algorithms. They play a crucial role in interpreting EEG signals accurately. Artificial neural networks also took over, providing real-time solutions to the colossal task of interpreting brain signals.

7.3. Towards the 21st Century

As we transitioned into the 21st century, the trajectory of BCI innovation reached an incline like never before. In 2000, Cyberkinetics, a US company, developed BrainGate, one of the first commercial BCIs. The system used an invasive technique and a sensor placed on the motor cortex to move a cursor and even robotic arms.

The mid-2000s witnessed another significant progress: electrodes on the surface of the brain – a technique known as electrocorticography (ECoG). ECoG demonstrated a superior spatial resolution and signal quality, pushing BCIs to a potential clinical application albeit requiring a surgical procedure.

The 2010s introduced us to Emotiv EPOC, a low-cost EEG-based BCI. This brought BCI technology to the consumer forefront for the first time. Innovations like Neurosky MindWave further capitalized on this trend and made consumer-grade BCIs a reality. These devices found applications in gaming, meditation, and academics.

7.4. Recent Developments: Neuromodulation Techniques

The present decade is witnessing rapid advances in neuromodulation techniques for BCI, such as Transcranial Magnetic Stimulation (TMS), and transcranial Direct Current Stimulation (tDCS). These non-invasive techniques aim to modulate brain activity, promising potential therapeutic applications in neurorehabilitation and mental disorder treatments.

7.5. Future Trends of BCIs

Looking into the future, there are two main directions. On one hand, neuroprosthetics and BCIs for medical purposes continue to advance, utilizing invasive techniques for improved results despite higher risk. On the other hand, non-invasive BCIs are moving closer to the consumer market, with companies like Neurable working on BCI enabled virtual reality systems.

Finally, the disruptive potential held by BCI technology cannot be overstated. As we move forward into uncharted territories, we stand witness to a future wherein seamless communication between the brain and machines would become just another facet of day-to-day life, altering our interaction with technology at a fundamental level.

In conclusion, from a few scattered research efforts in laboratories to the cusp of mainstream fruition, BCI technology has come a long way. This evolution is the result of countless dedicated researchers who envisioned and endeavored towards what seemed impossible just a few decades ago. The field of BCI is undoubtedly a living testament to how technology, when intertwined with ingenuity and resiliency, can create a seismic shift in our lives.

Chapter 8. Navigating the Challenges: Limitations and Solutions

A journey into any pioneering realm of technology always involves surmounting a series of challenges, and Brain-Computer Interfaces (BCIs) are no exception to this rule. Presently, BCIs are grappling with limitations primarily pertaining to their system components, reliability of signal detection and transmission, patient safety, and ethical issues. Simultaneously, a nexus of talented scientists and researchers are relentlessly exploring solutions to alleviate these challenges.

8.1. Technological and System Limitations

BCIs are a dramatic amalgamation of neurology, computer science, and biomedical engineering. Each of these components presents a unique set of challenges. From signal detection and preprocessing to feature extraction, translation algorithm, and output device control, each step in a BCI system represents a potential ground for limitations.

The task of collecting high-resolution neural signals alone is an arduous undertaking. Available techniques like Electroencephalography (EEG), Magnetoencephalography (MEG), or Functional Magnetic Resonance Imaging (fMRI) come with their individual pitfalls. EEG, for instance, suffers from poor spatial resolution, whereas fMRI produces significant temporal lag.

Once the signals are collected, there is the crucial process of preprocessing which involves filtering, signal-to-noise enhancement, and baseline correction. Difficulty arises in maintaining the integrity of the signal during these steps as each comes with possible distortions.

Further down the line, classification and machine learning techniques adopted for signal feature extraction and translation algorithms can influence the efficiency of the BCI system. Herein, maintaining system robustness and adaptability remains a considerable challenge.

Lastly, the task of mapping and translating neural signals into commands for external devices, such as computers or prosthetics, also comes with inherent difficulties ranging from lag time to incorrect execution.

8.2. Overcoming Technological and System Limitations

In response to the aforementioned technological and systemic limitations, continuous advancements are being made in the field. There are recurrent endeavors towards improving the quality of imaging technology and neural signal collection methods, focused on enhancing the signal-to-noise ratio and reducing temporal lag and interferences.

Further, innovative machine learning techniques are continuously being developed and implemented to improve the interpretation of brain signals. Efforts are also underway to ensure increased system adaptability that could self-update according to the user's needs and behavior.

There is a rising trend to use 'hybrid BCIs' which combine two or more different BCI paradigms or integrate a BCI system with other systems to increase overall system performance.

8.3. Safety and Ethical Considerations

The safety of BCI users is paramount, and this prioritization is a major challenge for persistent researchers. The implantation process for invasive BCIs is laden with numerous inherent risks. Complications may range from minor infections to severe neurological conditions, adding to the current limitations.

Furthermore, BCIs touch sensitive ethical areas, primarily due to their intimate interaction with human cognition. Issues of privacy, identity alteration, and mental autonomy surface when we delve into this territory.

8.4. Addressing Safety and Ethical Concerns

Safety issues surrounding BCIs call for continuous refinement of the procedures involved, surgical and otherwise. Surgical advancements that diminish risks associated with implantation processes are actively sought after.

In terms of ethics, a framework addressing privacy concerns, legislation for BCI usage and proper education of users about potential risks and implications is needed. By fostering an open dialogue on the ethical implications, we can anticipate problems and sort them before they turn insurmountable.

8.5. The Road Ahead

The challenges facing Brain-Computer Interfaces are indeed significant, but they don't overshadow the immense potential they hold. Neuroprosthetics, neurorehabilitation, cognition enhancement are only some of the arenas that BCI technology promises to revolutionize.

Conquering these hurdles will require persistent interdisciplinary collaboration, combining the expertise of neuroscientists, engineers, computer scientists, ethicists, and clinicians. Moreover, recognizing these challenges should serve as motivation to explore the unchartered territories that the universe of BCIs presents.

As we continue to navigate this intricate labyrinth of BCI limitations and solutions, we bear witness to the relentless human quest for progress. And it is within such pioneering spirit, couched in diligent scientific inquiry and ethical consciousness, that the true potential of BCIs will unfurl and flourish in the years to come.

Chapter 9. In the Realm of Ethics: Balancing Innovation and Equity

Brain-computer interfaces (BCIs) are a thrilling example of technology's potential to change lives. As we strive to push the boundaries of human ability, it's essential to remember that behind each wave of innovation is a range of ethical considerations. In this section, we chart the intricate balance between breakthroughs in this field and the ethical landscape we must navigate as we develop and implement these transformative tools.

9.1. Equity in Access and Affordability

First and foremost, equity in access and affordability must be a cornerstone of any discussions related to BCIs. While the potential benefits of BCIs are indeed ground-breaking, we must recognize the disparity in global resource allocation. Advanced healthcare technologies and techniques often come with prohibitively high costs that can exacerbate pre-existing inequities in society.

Essentially, the development of these advanced technologies should follow a principle of distributive justice, aiming for the fair distribution of benefits and burdens. This requires a concerted effort by policy-makers, industry, healthcare providers, and patient advocacy organizations to work cooperatively in addressing affordability and access.

9.2. Consent and Autonomy

Questions of consent and autonomy lie at the heart of BCI ethics. The use of BCI technology can potentially infringe upon individual's right to self-determination and privacy. Can one adequately comprehend and give informed consent for a procedure that involves such a complex interplay of medical, psychological, and social factors?

Moreover, what happens if the individual, once fitted with a BCI, changes their mind? The possibility of reversal, adjusting, or removing implants is a significant issue, particularly when considering the invasive nature of some BCI technologies.

The principle of respect for autonomy demands clearly defined and user-friendly protocols that allow individuals to both understand the repercussions of BCI use and make informed decisions about their healthcare.

9.3. Responsible Innovation and Safety Regulations

Safety regulations surrounding BCI devices may seem stifling to innovation, but they play a vital role in ensuring that technological advances do not break ethical bounds. BCIs, particularly invasive ones, come with significant health risks, including infection and adverse neurological effects.

In the pursuit of technological progress and improved quality of life for users, the onus is on the researchers, healthcare providers, and industry innovators to adhere to a stringent testing regime and robust regulatory framework. Regular review and update of standards on design, implementation, and post-implant management of BCIs must be rigorously upheld. The concept of responsible innovation encapsulates this ethos well, coalescing progress and ethics in a sustainable manner.

9.4. Privacy and Data Protection

BCIs deal with the most intimate of information – our thoughts. Consequently, privacy and data protection are crucial concerns. Without proper safeguards, sensitive neurological data transmitted from BCIs could become a gold mine for data miners and potential misuse. Regulatory measures must be established to protect users' privacy and guard against unauthorized access, sharing, or misuse of data.

9.5. Cognitive Liberty and Identity

On a deeper level, we must tackle the philosophical and psychological aspects of BCI use. Cognitive liberty and identity challenges arise because BCIs can potentially change our perception, thoughts, and personalities. What happens when a technology has the power to influence our mind or alter our physical capabilities?

This profound question should trigger careful analysis of the interplay between human identity and technological enhancement. While the primary intention of BCIs is to restore or augment human abilities, it is crucial to evaluate the impact on a user's selfhood, personal identity, and societal inclusion. Cognitive liberty, or the right to mental self-determination, should thus form a part of ethical deliberations alongside physical autonomy.

Despite being relatively new territory, the ethical landscape surrounding BCI use is crucial to negotiate. Balancing technological progress with ethical considerations must always remain paramount. From access and affordability to cognitive liberty and identity, a holistic understanding of the ethical implications of BCIs will ensure a future where this powerful technology effectively serves humanity in an equitable and conscientious manner.

Chapter 10. Looking Ahead: Predicted Developments in BCI Technology

In the ever-evolving field of Brain-Computer Interfaces (BCIs), tomorrow promises not only to sustain but continually revolutionize the nature of human cognition and interactive abilities. As we embark on this voyage of forecasting, it is essential to keep in mind that these projections are rooted in current and emerging trends and scientific understandings.

10.1. The Blurring Boundaries: Merging of Human Intelligence and Artificial Intelligence

As technology progresses, we're gradually witnessing an eroding distinction between human intelligence and artificial intelligence (AI). Today, even rudimentary BCIs seamlessly interact with AI-based software, an integration that is poised to refine further. To put this into perspective, AI has exhibited impeccable accuracy and consistency in tasks that overwhelm the human brain—data analysis and pattern recognition, for instance.

How do they connect, and why does it matter in BCIs? The answer lies in the symbiosis shared between these two entities. BCIs record and interpret neural signals, while AI processes these signals, generating a human-like response or action. This synergy will evolve further, leading to high-end BCIs that mirror human responses more accurately and promptly, thus making BCIs more intuitive and more personalized.

10.2. The Surge of Neuroprosthetics

Neuroprosthetics represent a significant breakthrough in BCI technology. By replicating or replacing a part of the individual's nervous system, these prosthetics facilitate normal or near-normal functioning. Today, we see this primarily in applications related to mobility, where prosthetics mimic complex actions like grabbing, holding or walking.

In the future, expect these to extend further. The potential for neuroprosthetics technology is vast, enabling life-like replication of sensory and motor functions—a prosthetic arm that can feel temperature or texture, or a prosthetic leg that can sense distance and pressure. The enhanced feedback loop and growing refinement in sensor technology will fundamentally alter the way neuroprosthetics are designed, advancing their integration into the human body.

10.3. Non-Invasive BCIs

Current BCI systems often involve the use of invasive methodologies for signal capture, requiring surgical interventions. However, non-invasive BCI technologies are rapidly developing. Electroencephalography (EEG)-based systems have proliferated in recent years, presenting a less risky option for potential users.

Advancements in these systems foresee a future where BCIs will be as ubiquitous as smartphones—serving not only medical needs but also enhancing daily human life. From mood regulation and fostering learning progress to fine-tuning athlete performance and aiding in meditation, the prospects expand as we continue to discern the brain's enigmatic language.

10.4. Tailoring Connectivity: Personalized BCIs

As with any technology tied to individuals, there is an urgent and rising need for personalization. BCIs, too, are no exception. Each individual has a unique neural signature, and hence BCIs of the future will be tailored to match these unique brain patterns.

Deep learning algorithms, a subset of machine learning, are expected to lead this trend. By analyzing and learning from an individual's brain data, these algorithms can then generate models tailored to the user's cognitive patterns, thus evolving BCIs to become individual-specific interfaces.

10.5. Ethical Considerations and Regulatory Frameworks

As BCIs permeate more aspects of daily life and medical treatments, ethical and regulatory considerations will become prominent. Questions concerning data privacy, user autonomy, access to, and control of personal neurological data will need addressing.

Regulatory bodies might establish frameworks to assess the safety and efficacy of novel BCI applications. This landscape would not only involve scientists and policy-makers but also require active participation from ethicists, sociologists, and end-users.

10.6. The Advent of Neuralnanorobotics

Neuralnanorobotics represents the frontier of BCI technology—tiny, programmable machines capable of interaction and manipulation at a cellular level. While still an area of ongoing research, the potential implications are immense: neuralnanorobots could one day facilitate the transmission of information directly from the brain to digital devices, creating an ultimate brain-computer interface.

Our journey into the future of BCI technology, while rooted in current understanding and realistic speculation, is still diverse and thrilling. The beauty of technology and innovation is its inherent unpredictability—making one thing certain, BCIs will become an intimate part of the human experience. We step into a future where the boundaries between biology and technology blend, creating a world ripe for exploration and unimaginable innovation.

Chapter 11. Conclusion: The Augmenting Human Potential

As the curtain closes on this thrilling exploration of Brain-Computer Interfaces (BCIs), the true essence of this technological marvel becomes ever more apparent. Far from being a fringe science fiction trope, BCIs denote a tangible and transformative marriage of neurology, computer science, and biomedical engineering that holds the potential to revolutionize numerous facets of human life.

11.1. The Promise of Tomorrow

BCIs, although not yet commonplace, have already demonstrated how they can fundamentally alter the way we approach disabilities and neurological disorders. Imagine a world where paralysis could be overcome, where locked-in patients can communicate, and where amputees can regain their sense of touch through neuroprosthetics. These possibilities aren't distant science fiction scenarios; they are around the corner, made accessible through ongoing research and development in the realm of BCIs.

Over the horizon looms the potential for cognitive augmentation. Future versions of BCIs could allow us to access memories and information faster, process new information more efficiently, and even learn skills overnight. Theoretically, it could enable a form of hypercognition, creating a human intellect enhanced to levels so far only dreamed of in our boldest literature and cinema.

11.2. The Power of Balance

However, as with most potent technologies, BCIs hold the power for both awe-inspiring benefits and potent drawbacks. It is essential to strike a careful balance between human advancement and ethical considerations. In our pursuit for cognitive augmentation and overcoming physical limitations, we must remember the fundamental principles that define us as human beings. This includes maintaining our autonomy, privacy, and ensuring equal access to such advancements.

The potential threats to personal privacy posed by BCIs cannot be ignored. In a world where thoughts can be read, and potentially manipulated, there must be stringent safeguards put in place to protect the sanctity of our inner selves. We should not let our rush for progress blind us to the fact that our minds, the source of our thoughts, emotions, and perception of reality, are still our own.

Equally, the risk of a widening divide between those who have access to this technology and those who do not is very real. We must take steps to ensure that BCIs, like all technology, must not become tools of inequality. They should be used to advance humanity as a whole, not just a privileged few.

11.3. Steering the Course

BCIs represent a new era in technology and medicine, blending seamlessly to create opportunities beyond our comprehension. The research and investment in this field over the last few decades is finally blooming, and the fruits of labor are now within our grasp. However, the charge to augmenting human cognitive and sensory motor abilities with brain-machine integration must be made ethically and responsibly.

Responsibility spans from the researchers creating these interfaces, the governments regulating their use, and the society adapting to evolve with them. As with any transformative technology, the pitfalls of BCIs are of equal importance to its possibilities. Missteps along this journey could lead to irrevocable consequences, underscoring the need for comprehensive ethical and legislative frameworks surrounding BCI use.

11.4. The Final Frontier

In the final analysis, the advent of BCIs represents one more frontier in humanity's journey of technological advancement. As with any frontier, there are opportunities for enormous gains and unparalleled discoveries, but also the potential for serious risks and dangers. And just like the pioneers before us, we must meet these challenges head-on, with a blend of optimism, realism, and respect for the tremendous power we hold.

Through our exploration of BCIs, we glimpse future trends and potential applications, starting from their humble beginnings to the groundbreaking applications in neuroprosthetics, and the challenges they pose. We find ourselves at the dawn of a brave new world where mind and machine intrinsically intermingle in ways previously relegated to the spheres of imagination and invention.

BCIs promise a future where human cognition, communication, and sensory motor systems can be amplified to a level we've never known. As we move into this future, though, we need to remember that despite our technological prowess, we remain human - with all the complexity that entails. It is this balance that will allow us to advance into a positive and inclusive future, rather than an Orwellian dystopia.

In the balance of this promise and peril rests our greatest challenge - creating a future that takes the best of what BCIs can offer, while tempering their potential to disrupt. It's a challenge that may define the course of humanity's evolution well into the 21st century and beyond. But, well-guided by thoughtfulness, responsibility, and a profound respect for our shared humanity, we can rise to meet it. The story of BCI is just beginning, its most exciting chapters are yet to be written, and we are the protagonists of that narrative. The future of this enthralling synthesis awaits our discerning navigation. The pen is poised; let's script this epic tale together, thoughtfully, responsibly, and advantageously.

www.ingramcontent.com/pod-product-compliance
Lightning Source LLC
LaVergne TN
LVHW051634050326
832903LV00033B/4752